Celebrating Your Church Anniversary

Foreword

For Christian people, church anniversaries can have something of the joy and glory, in their own dimension, that personal birthdays or wedding anniversaries can have. It is a splendid dimension, indeed, for these occasions celebrate God's work with his people. How fortunate we are, then, to have a practical book on church anniversaries from a pastor who has been involved and challenged by several of them in the course of his pastoral experience. From my own labors in writing the history of his present church, and from my knowledge gained when I was also privileged to minister to it, I can testify to his thoughtful, careful, and imaginative attention to the planning and the conduct of the events by which he led his people through the celebration of the church's 150 years of life. He believes, and we can all believe with him, that such a time of remembrance can prove itself to be a God-given means of the renewal of a church. His book should find a warm welcome with every pastor (and any lay person) who sees an anniversary just ahead. God bless the mission of this book!

John Woolman Brush

Contents

Preface

When a church honestly assesses its ministry as the lengthened shadow of a Person who walked the earth some centuries ago, it quickly sees its own many defects and constant need of the Master's strength and direction. The celebration of an anniversary, far from being merely glorious, is a humbling, challenging experience that spurs one to greater endeavor. Every detail of a celebration, from dream to consummation and the hope it engenders for the future, progresses toward the anticipation that on both church and individual may fall the blessing of the Lord, as though he were saying, "Well done, good and faithful workmen; enter into the joy of your Lord."

I am grateful for the happenstances which caused my pastorates to fall in churches that had anniversaries to be celebrated. My unusual experience includes the celebration of four major anniversaries: the one hundredth in the First Baptist Church, Rockville, Connecticut; the one hundred fiftieth in the First Baptist Church, Middletown, Connecticut; the fiftieth in City Park Baptist Church, Denver, Colorado; and the one hundred fiftieth in the First Baptist Church of New Haven, Connecticut. In addition, I have been chairman of various committees that planned statewide summer camp anniversaries in Colorado and Connecticut, and it was my privilege to give leadership and direction to the centennial celebration of the Connecticut Valley Hospital.

Moreover, a weather eye has been maintained through the years on modes and practices of other denominations and churches that sought to pay their respect to the past and gain strength for the present and future. Some of these were a two hundred twenty-fifth Congregational celebration, a two hundred fiftieth anniversary of Christ Episcopal Church, Boston, and the three hundredth anniversary of the First Baptist Church of Boston.

I am sincerely indebted to scores of people in the churches, who entered enthusiastically into the tune-up processes of readying and consolidating the celebrations which meant so much to their churches. City and state secretaries, pastors, and laymen all over the United States have cheerfully responded to my many inquiries about the celebration of anniversaries and how to make them stimulating, spiritual, and generally profitable.

In particular, I would like to thank Dr. Ford Lewis Battles, Professor of Church History and History of Doctrine at Pittsburgh Theological Seminary, for his permission to include the "Checklist for a Historical Inventory of a Local Church" in the Appendix of this book.

In a large measure, this is a "how-to" book, containing many suggestions for effective ways to treasure the past, to rejoice in the present witness, and to face with courage the uncertain future. Even more, the book is a statement which points to the opportunities, the tools with which to work, and the thrill of fashioning an occasion of uniqueness, beauty, excellence, and significance. It shows how to seize upon the opportunity to receive with appreciation an inheritance, and to create out of the heritage something new which can be passed on. This paves the way for the enduring hope in the best that is yet to be!

Bacon's observation that "some books are to be tasted, others to be swallowed, and some few to be chewed and digested," when broken into its parts, applies to different portions of this book. For example, the chapters "Church Anniversaries Are Fun," "What Is a Significant Anniversary?" "Telling the Story (Publicity)," and "Summary and Sampling of Anniversaries" may well be tasted for their flavor and desirability. The chapters on planning for the coming anniversary and the process of founding, organizing, building, moving, and merging must be swallowed. Detailed suggestions in other chapters are to be chewed and digested.

This book urges the celebration of church anniversaries as means of stimulating and renewing the church. A general plan for the anniversary is offered. Thinking and feeling about the anniversary celebration must be given time to grow and develop. We are dealing with a moment in time, and a time schedule leading to, observing, and consolidating the event must be arranged and followed. Historical research naturally leads to the writing of a history, and the history leads to a pageant, timely exhibits, period costumes, special programs, and other events. There is development from one idea to another. Detailed instructions then follow, including suggestions that are so framed as to enable each church to formulate a set of goals and plans under which to accomplish its own mission.

If this book helps a few churches to achieve a fresh and vital understanding of their mission through the celebration of anniversaries it shall have accomplished a high purpose. It is sent forth in that hope.

ALVIN D. JOHNSON

New Haven
September 1, 1968.

1

Church Anniversaries Are Fun

Church anniversaries are fun. I have found them to be so, after living through several anniversary experiences. Amid the excitement of preparing for his church's one hundred fiftieth anniversary celebration, one deacon shared his exuberance with his relatives in Scotland. He was deflated when they failed to be impressed and informed him that their church had just celebrated its five hundredth anniversary! But it is not necessary to wait that long before having the joy of giving homage to those who had a vision and who experienced the prayer, pain, and satisfaction of doing a good work for their God and their fellows, both past and present.

A business man responded to the opportunity of giving his share toward the building of a new synagogue. When the project was completed, he discovered that he had given three times the amount he had originally intended to give. Some of his joy is revealed in his statement: "It isn't everyone who has the opportunity to help to build a synagogue in his lifetime!" Neither is it everyone who has the opportunity to help to celebrate a church anniversary, and thus to rejoice in a heritage that is unearned and undeserved.

Church anniversaries are not only fun, but they may well become the fulcrum on which a church can move into new areas of ministry. Add to this a new appreciation of the past, a more vital grasp of the present, and a new confidence for the future, and the possibilities of this coming event take on new significance for the total life and witness of the church.

There is a wealth of fun and fellowship for the church as it plans for and carries through a celebration. A period dress night, for example, will bring surprises and smiles. Deacons in Prince Albert coats and ladies wearing their grandmothers' dresses will provoke a light and pleasant spirit which contributes to the understanding of the past and a closer fellowship in the present. Parishioners of one church were delighted to see their pastor and his wife drive up in a horse and buggy during a two hundredth anniversary celebration. Of course, their costumes were in keeping with the mode of transportation. There is a transformation in people when they are dressed in clothes of yesteryear. New and interesting facets of personality are revealed.

There are fun and fellowship to be enjoyed also when a pageant is presented, for the past comes alive with familiar faces. If there is an historical display of old pictures, programs, and other items, eyes will light up and tongues will be loosened in remembrances of the days "when."

The return of old friends and pastors to the homecoming or banquet provides the opportunity for the renewal of old acquaintances, and names which have become legend now become personified. There is a continual heightening of Christian joy by this search into the past and detailed examination of the rich roots from which the present fellowship grows.

Church anniversaries are fun, not only in the entertainment sense but in the serious business of planning and celebrating the anniversary. The joy of the early disciples is reproduced by this depth living and witnessing of an anniversary year. Part of this discovered joy is in the increased sensi-

tivity to all age groups in the church fellowship and a sense that in years gone by, real people who faced real problems called on this fellowship to guide their children, to challenge their youth, and to comfort their aged and infirm.

Real joy comes from the intensity with which the church business is carried on because of the new perspective given by the approach of the events of the anniversary. First the spotlight is on the past, then upon the older members, then upon the vigorous core of the church, and finally upon the budding potential of the church's youth and children. The whole church, including its roots in the past, is examined sympathetically and in an understanding way. The future can be plotted with more certainty when evidences of God's leading and guidance in the past are uncovered.

The approach to the anniversary is a good time to re-examine the working of the committees and the boards of the church. How do they function? Does each board and committee understand and appreciate the contribution of the others? Does a new understanding of the diversity, yet the unity, in Christ become apparent in the accelerated functioning of the several groups during this crucial year of anniversary activity? Basically, an anniversary celebration does not dislocate the functions of a church, but the awareness of the people is aroused and the tempo of activity is increased. The anniversary year does not mean that the work of the various boards and committees has to be stopped or rerouted to let the anniversary train go through. Each board or committee functions more efficiently because all are interested in the progress of the particular part which is being contributed by that board or committee. The whole picture becomes more sharply etched and the richness of the fellowship enhanced. The hope is always present that, because of the gathered enthusiasm from the past, the present church might develop the strength to launch into new areas of adventurous witness and Christian living.

An anniversary is a good time for the boards and committees to focus their attention on a challenge target and to shoot for it with vigor and enthusiasm. Research shows what those in each group have contributed in the past. Each board and committee has the opportunity to realize the value of its function for the whole and in relation to the challenge of the Christ. From discovered evidences of sacrifice and goodwill new enthusiasms are generated to give a better witness for Christ in the present. There will be high humor and at the same time a savoring of the moment, for in the perspective of the past the present is seen as a passing phenomenon to be treasured.

Anniversary time is a time of joy for those who have put in their active day in the church work. It is a time to lift up individuals who have given much to the church and who, because of their advancing years, can no longer give as much as their spirits might dictate. Here is an example of a citation to honor one such individual during a centennial celebration:

MISS GERTRUDE HERSKELL

For loving, understanding, and worrying about (as you call them) "the little folks." For the countless miles you have walked to visit them; for the many notes and letters you have written; for the continued thought and planning, the interest and concern for the welfare of each one of these. For the regard and vision you have for the Church; for the consecrated service to this Church which has been passed on and through you by your parents, who were instrumental in the building of this Church building; for your continued prayers and many unknown contributions, spiritual and physical, we, the present Church, as a part of our Centennial Celebration desire that you have this public expression of our feelings and esteem, and that this statement be included in the church records for this year.

Another citation was presented to one in absentia. Miss Jennie Evans had been confined to her home for over a decade with crippling arthritis and yet she continued to make her Christian witness even in adversity. Her citation read:

> For your sweet Christianity which radiates from your pain-racked body; for the counsel and advice in things of the spirit; for your radiant Christian spirit which has been not weakened but strengthened by your years of suffering; for your triumphant Christian philosophy which is rooted and grounded in a dependable God, we . . . desire that you have this public expression of our feelings and esteem . . . and same be recorded. . . .

There is a joy in being thankful and giving thanks to those who are still on hand to appreciate it. Said one older person in gratitude, "Thank you; I'd rather smell the flowers of appreciation now. I cannot smell them on my grave."

An anniversary celebration offers the opportunity to memorialize some person or persons who are important in the life of the church. These may have been outstanding spiritual leaders, selfless Sunday church school teachers, or financial benefactors of the church and its program. A missionary, a minister, deacon, or deaconess, because of his length and/or depth of service, could be honored. Memorial offering and communion plates, pews, hymnbooks, bells, platform furniture, or windows may be dedicated; the suggested list is as long as an ecclesiologist's catalog.

At anniversary time, a book of remembrance is particularly in order. Previous gifts can be entered and plans made to continue the entries when gifts and bequests are made to the church. This is a record of memorials that serve and will continue to serve. The spirit and meaning of such a book is caught up in the inscription for the Book of Remembrance of the Grace Presbyterian Church of Jenkintown, Pennsylvania. It reads: "Grant that we whose lot is cast in so goodly a heritage may strive together the more abundantly to extend to others what we so richly enjoy." The biblical basis for a book of remembrance is shown by the quotation. "Then those who feared the Lord spoke with one another; the Lord heeded and heard them, and a book of remembrance was written before him of those who feared the Lord and thought on his name" (Malachi 3:16).

2

What Is a Significant Anniversary?

What is a significant anniversary celebration for a church fellowship? No one knows, really, except the local group. What is meaningful to one church is inapplicable to another. Even then, it is only when boards and committees meet and consider the total fellowship which spans the past and present, and looks into the future, that a significant celebration can be visualized. Generally speaking, a significant anniversary celebration pays respect to the past, assesses the present, and strides with vigor and courage into the future. A significant anniversary is a created mood, rather than a number of unrelated items attempted and accomplished. It is the increased sensitivity of a fellowship to its own calling and potential which makes them a part of the body of Christ in the world today. To be sure, activity and accomplishment are important, but a significant celebration is characterized more by a rediscovered sense of mission, humility, courage, and awe at the privilege of taking part in a great ongoing task.

Interwoven with and inseparable from this new sense of mission are the activities and accomplishments which go along with a successful observance, not neglecting to pay tribute to God-inspired individuals of the past who have followed the cloud by day and the pillar of fire by night.

There are six areas, types of activity, or facets of an anniversary celebration. These are general enough to apply to all fellowships, and they present the setting in which a unique celebration ond observance can be played with local actors and with a plot that grows out of the local situation. Here are the six areas.

1. *Research and write the history of the church.* This may be done by making use of previous research and written history, or it may mean going back to original documents, minutes, and records of the church. Of course, a study of the national and local historical background helps to put the church in its proper setting and measures the uniqueness of its effort and witness. Then, with this history as a foundation, a pageant may be considered.

2. *Prepare an exhibit of old pictures, programs, publications, awards, and other memorabilia.* These can be gathered from many sources. There's gold among the volume of trash in parishioners' attics and in forgotten places in the church building. Careful selection and orderly display bring a new dimension to the history of the fellowship.

3. *Set aside an evening, a week-long series of events, or a weekend as the high point in the anniversary year.*

4. *Assign to each particular group some month or event.* The peculiar contribution made by an organization can be uplifted and given an historical perspective. At the same time, an added emphasis can be given to its present value. For example, the board of deacons can emphasize its evangelistic responsibility by a visitation of every member and friend. A series of neighborhood meetings or a series of controversial or challenging films can be programmed to interest the community around the church. The board of Christian education, cooperating with the youth of the church, can produce a pageant from the history and present it.

5. *Conceive and execute some challenging event signifying the servant role of the church.* An example of such an emphasis may be seen in an act of the First Baptist Church in New Haven. During the three-day Connecticut Baptist Convention this church, despite some qualms and misgivings, played host, and thereby discovered hidden sources of

strength. On attractive anniversary posters all could read words expressing the offer of the congregation: WHAT CAN WE DO FOR YOU?

6. Devise long-range plans and foreseeable goals for the next few years. Such ideas could be formulated by various groups, boards, and committees, and presented for formal acceptance at the next annual meeting.

These six basic suggestions have emerged from actual anniversary situations and have proved their exciting qualities and worth. They do not hinder the unique expression of the local church, but they can provide a design and can help a church to seize the opportunities that present themselves when anniversary time rolls around. By uncovering and honestly examining its greatest need, a church may find the greatest opportunity and a realistic and challenging goal at which to aim. The anniversary will then be a unique celebration.

Anniversary activity at its best is penetration into the living core of the church. It can even call forth courage to attempt new areas and modes of ministry. It can challenge the church to rediscover the Christ-called and Christ-led fellowship into whose heritage the present generation has entered.

In Genesis 26 there is the story of Isaac digging again the wells of water which had been dug in the days of Abraham, his father. In this case, the wells had been filled with dirt and rubbish by the Philistines, and the springing water stopped. In a church's history, maybe the springing wells of spiritual water have been stopped by wars and rumors of wars, by depression or affluence, by the proliferation of power, speed, and noise. These are real enough, but when deep shafts of inquiry are sunk into the inner life and reality of the fellowship, then truly refreshing waters for parched spirits can be found. This inquiry into the past does not mean a cowardly retreat into old ways of doing things, but the search for life, strength, and energy which can then be fashioned and used in the business of living a life, and living it abundantly and with more significance today. The inquiry can also cause the reshaping of goals and the tapping of new sources of strength for the living of these days with courage and resolution. Such a search can bring the new establishment of goals, and a challenge to the congregation to resist the natural attraction of secular things and times, and also to aim at the spiritual goals that are inherent in Christ.

Anniversary activity does not call for a slavish worship of the past nor a return to archaic forms of speech, dress, or fashion. It means attuning the present generation to those values which do not change and which give direction and meaning to life for the individual and the society in which he lives, as well as to worldwide society as it seeks brotherhood and understanding.

A significant anniversary celebration can be experienced through prayer, intelligent planning, and vigorous execution. And maybe there is a kernel of truth in James Russell Lowell's lines, "Not failure, but low aim, is crime." Some things do not become obsolete: justice, mercy, kindness, love. These truths are ever new and challenging. These are the ties that can bind a world together. Indeed, if the world does not learn to live in community based on these truths, there is a good chance that there will be no world.

3

On the Way

A church is on the way toward a successful anniversary celebration when it becomes conscious of the anniversary date months, or even years, before it arrives. An *early, slow* start is wise. Plenty of time should be allowed for the idea to become firmly planted in the minds of the people. It is best not to hurry or force the thinking and decision-making of the congregation. Like gardens, anniversaries should be conceived, planned, planted, cultivated, and harvested. The seeds need time to grow and mature before they can be harvested. Only after the climate has been established is the church ready to make specific plans and programs.

One technique in enlisting the interest of the people in a celebration is to ask them to share the names of those who might be interested in receiving an invitation to return to a "Homecoming." Of course, every component of the usual church news media can be used to let the coming event become known. The successful celebration is one that is conducted by the people. It is both interesting and heartwarming to witness the rising enthusiasm as each person takes his part in planning for and contributing to the celebration.

When the people have become sufficiently excited about conducting a celebration, the next step is to discover what such a celebration should be like for their own church, for no two churches are alike. Perhaps the best procedure at this point is that of brainstorming. A brainstorm is a sudden bright idea, and sometimes a harebrained idea. A small group of people begin to think about a specific subject. Each person frankly and impulsively says whatever comes to his mind about the subject. Every statement is recorded; and no statement is to be regarded as too rash, outlandish, or foolhardy to be put into the record.

Brainstorming on a set of questions that are especially related to anniversary celebrations can be used in all the boards, committees, societies, and other groups throughout the church. When representative groups begin to conduct brainstorming sessions on anniversary opportunities, the excitement mounts and the pace and planning undergo acceleration. These sessions, with their appeal to the thinking and suggestions of everyone, cultivate the atmosphere in which the greatest wisdom and excellence can be brought to focus on the kind of anniversary celebration which best fits the needs and opportunities of the particular church in which they are held. A list of possible questions follows:

1. Why have an anniversary celebration?
2. What meaning does it or can it have?
3. Who is challenged by an anniversary?
4. What can we expect to accomplish by remembering the past?
5. What bearing can this introspection have on the present and the future?
6. How much of what we enjoy in our church has resulted from the labor of others?
7. Why were people interested in beginning a work of the Lord in this place?
8. Are there evidences of sacrifice and good stewardship which resulted in this testimony to God's leading?

9. How would a fresh sensitivity to the "cloud of witnesses" of former years strengthen our witness today?

10. How can an anniversary be an adventure and fun?

In a sense, this whole book is an answer to these questions. Experience over many years has shown that these brainstorming questions will be answered in certain ways. The following are some of the ideas that might be expected to emerge:

1. An anniversary celebration is a way of saying "thank you" to the past. The present owes this much to the past.

2. The sense of continuity becomes real, and the present is not isolated from either the past or the future.

3. Young, old, men, women, boards, committees, and other groups — the whole church — take notice of an historic dimension which is too often lost to sight because of the business of the present or the scramble for the future.

4. The fundamentals of living in community — justice, kindness, humility, love, preferring one another — are fostered. The salt gets back its savor, and the worldwide areas of need and the responsibility of the church are brought into focus.

5. A more realistic assessment of the present as a part of the continuum emerges, and the necessity to build carefully today for tomorrow is emphasized.

6. Although the evidence of labor and sacrifice performed in the past is visibly revealed in a building or an endowment, it soon becomes clear that the greater intangibles of tradition, faith, and spiritual heritage are the treasures that are passed on from generation to generation.

7. People labored in this place because they felt the leading of God. In view of this, the current generation is prompted to ask: What is God's leading for us today?

8. Such legacies as buildings, trust funds, missionary outreach over the years, a Sunday church school, and helpful worship services through war, depression, and affluence; challenge to youth to enter church-related vocations; care for the elderly and the exceptional child; and the pastoral and

diaconal ministrations over the years are evidences of spiritual fervor, sacrifice, and good stewardship.

9. The witness of the church today would be strengthened by the knowledge that it follows in a noble company, that it has the sole responsibility for a vital witness in word and deed today without which there will be no "faith of our fathers" tomorrow. Is not the Christian faith always but one generation from extinction?

10. The best planning and effort should go into the anniversary celebration. Adventure and fellowship will come as delightful surprises. Joy characterized the early disciples; it should characterize the anniversary from beginning to end.

Sometimes a church is prevented from beginning preparations for a celebration by an obstacle, such as a pastoral change, difficult times, or just plain neglect of the anniversary date. In such a case, the optimum amount of time for planning and preparation is curtailed. However, the celebration need not be abandoned. Even though preparation and planning are highly important, and longer, more balanced planning is much to be desired, all is not lost.

It is not too late to plan even when the anniversary year has arrived, for it often happens that the effect of the celebration is felt most strongly after the anniversary year has passed. Such effects are seen in increased attendance, a greater aliveness and sensitivity to the things of the spirit; and indeed, the whole functioning of the church moves to a higher plane. The mission of stewardship and evangelism takes on new meaning because of the anniversary planning and celebration. Hence, it may be said that *the proper time for a celebration is when the local group is ready and prepared.* Any church can get a new lease on life by reexamining its roots. In so doing it rejoices in its existence and aspires to a greater witness for Christ in the future.

When interested workers are needed for a contemplated anniversary celebration, there are several kinds of letters that are useful. The following sample letters will be found in full in the Appendix, pages 85-89:

1. Announcement of the coming anniversary.
2. Request to serve on the Anniversary Committee.
3. Gratitude for acceptance of assignment on committee.
4. Appeal for funds for the anniversary.
5. Invitation to members and friends to attend the anniversary banquet.
6. Letter of thanks to all anniversary workers.

Every letter should be individually written, and signed personally by the chairman of the committee or the pastor. Only first class postage should be used. For the best kind of response, enclose a stamped, self-addressed envelope or card. Any kind of shortcut will give the impression that the anniversary is a second-class affair, and the response will be treated in kind.

The anniversary endeavor is a privilege for all who take part and leads to great fun and fellowship. Indeed, this is an important by-product of an anniversary. Growing enthusiasm, humor, and increased fellowship spring up, especially between the older and younger members of the church. Scurrying around for appropriate costumes, borrowing them, making them, and renting them are all part of the fun. Everyone will see another side of solemn Deacon Jones when he is

dressed in clothes of yesteryear; or of Mrs. Jones when she jubilantly appears in frills and laces.

The fun to be had in a pageant will abundantly pay for the time and effort in preparing it. The role-playing will tie the past to the present and the present to the past. The present woman's society may portray the role of a former group of ladies who were knitting socks and sweaters for the doughboys of World War I. A pageant gives reality to a bygone era which can be seen in no other way, and certainly with no greater fun.

In a more serious vein, a narrator can read the record of a certain thrilling event in the history of the church while spotlights are aimed at a tableau of costumed figures portraying those in the past who courageously declared: "Here I stand; I can do no other." Audience and actors alike are impressed with the depths of spiritual commitment and the price paid by those of the past. But in addition a new dimension has been added to the present, and there is the feeling that other groups, perhaps sometime in the dim future, will also be called to courageous living.

Through the anniversary celebration the present generation will gain an increased appreciation of the lasting contributions of the past generations. In spite of the changing modes of life, as the present judges the past so will the present be judged—not by success alone, but by loyalty and steadfastness in the midst of storm. The members of the church of the present will be stimulated to abound in the work of the Lord in their day in order to pass on a worthy legacy to those in the future.

4

Costs and Financing

Any worthwhile endeavor justifies the spending of money. A church that plans for an anniversary will therefore wrestle with the problem of financing. After the people of the church have become enthusiastic about the prospects of a celebration, it is wise for both pastor and people to face frankly the fact that there will be costs.

What should be the cost of a significant anniversary? Some examples of justified expenses are an honorarium for the historian, the cost of printing the history, special speakers, including the cost of their transportation, special guests at the banquet, the printing of programs, pictures for publicity, and helping large families to pay for banquet tickets. The list grows, but the church's interest is also growing as plans develop. The problem of cost must be assessed, but the amount can partially be determined by the thoroughness with which the church desires to celebrate its birthday. For the joy before it, the church will find the means. When people want something badly enough, they will pay for it gladly. Here is an opportunity to teach the joys of good stewardship.

Faith should govern the financial planning for the anniversary. The money may not be in hand, but it will come. Should the people desire to go through with a significant program, they can find a way of financing what they want to do. If a church has survived long enough to reach an anniversary, the group has had to wrestle many times with money problems. When finances are regarded in this way, they can be a challenge rather than a damper. Doesn't an ambitious goal reflect optimism, which is a mark of the Christian outlook? Taken in stride, the financial undergirding of the special events will add relish to the whole of the proceedings. Good stewardship seems to indicate that a church anniversary should not be subsidized by the financial achievements of the past nor should the present effort put a burdensome mortgage on the future.

The most orderly way to raise the money for the celebration is to include an amount in the church budget, to be raised in addition to the regular ongoing expenses of the church. This shows a need and stimulates the greater giving that helps to underwrite the expenses of the anniversary year.

There are those in the church who would rather make a single cash payment or a series of cash payments by check than support the celebration by any other method. These individual or group sponsors of the anniversary program are to be congratulated and encouraged to make their contributions early.

A special offering envelope for the anniversary should be prepared and distributed generally among members and friends of the church. (See the Appendix for suggested size, makeup, and wording.)

In two celebrations, mite boxes were used effectively. In one case, these were pint-sized containers with a picture wrapper of the church. In the other, they were clear plastic containers in which a colored picture postcard of the church was placed. These mite boxes can be made by assembly-line production at a special church meeting and fun can be had

in their making as well as in their filling. In one of these situations, almost two thousand dollars were raised by this method. The collecting was dramatized by placing the coin-filled containers in an antique horsehide trunk found in the church. The little mite box gets the interest of the people who would not think in terms of writing a check or making a large contribution.

Other interesting devices for stimulating contributions are the production of a silver spoon with the anniversary date, a plate made for the occasion, a tile containing a picture of the church, church stationery, or church postcards. All of these are items which are regarded by the people as mementos of the anniversary.

Banquets always cost more than the mere expense of the food and service. In order to cover all expenses adequately, it is wise to add a small percentage to the estimated cost to be shared by each anniversary banquet ticket, so as to defray the costs of guest tickets and unexpected items, such as the renting of equipment, dishes, chairs, and tables.

In one anniversary the publishing of a history of the church was the main expense. A professional historian was engaged to do the research and writing, and the history was published in a handsome, hard-cover volume. A good part of the expense was met by a number of sponsors who contributed five dollars or more for the publication of the book. Then the sale of the book helped to balance the outgo with the income. A special occasion when the author was present for an autograph party was no small help in making ends meet.

Just how any church can raise enough money for a significant anniversary only the people of that church can determine. Here again is an opportunity for a group of people to see a problem as an opportunity, assess the necessity for some creative approach, then with vigor and zeal attack the problem. As usual, the more people concerned with the problem and the more working for its solution, the easier the solution will become. The experiences of anniversaries with different congregations of people has shown that the financial phase of the anniversary takes care of itself very well when the way is opened for people to respond to the need.

More important than undergirding the anniversary program with adequate finances is the financial challenge which an anniversary can be. The celebration can be the platform for a financial campaign for writing off the mortgage, funding a new addition, gaining the base for a staff increase, or providing for a new missionary work in another part of the community or the world. It can be the moment of truth when the present church looks at itself in the light of the past, which also had its moments of challenge and courageous decision and action. The anniversary year may be the time when a budget increase can become a possibility, and a new level of ministry enjoyed for years to come. The anniversary year may be compared with the first year of the church, and an attempt made to equal or surpass the sacrifices that were then necessary for a fellowship and fulfillment of a mission.

Of course, in any such comparison, the differences between the ways of life then and those of the present must be assessed and judged. Travel, communication, and financing have all been revolutionized by modern technology. The assessment is humbling and challenging. The pioneer efforts made in a bygone day are a challenge for the present day. If in the assessment the church comes to realize that the greatest possession is a consuming love for God and man and a faith, not in man-made plans and schemes, but first, last, and always in a living, leading Christ, then a new vigor will characterize the entry into tomorrow.

The old truth still works: "Seek first his [God's] kingdom and his righteousness" in the observance of the anniversary celebration, and the means will be forthcoming.

5

Analyzing the Celebration

A department store has many items from which to choose. As the customer browses, he finds items he needs and wants. Sometimes the display stimulates desires the customer did not have when he entered the store. He may see an item displayed which will satisfy a need or fancy of which he had been unaware at the time he entered the store.

The following specific suggestions are like the items displayed in a store for examination. Maybe a person will not want some of the items suggested, or perhaps he may be stimulated by a particular suggestion to adapt it to his own situation. Reading this chapter will be a kind of window-shopping by which one may get to know the fashion of the moment and still remain free to buy or not to buy according to his own need and resources. These suggestions are made for the purpose of stimulating the creativity of the reader rather than to lay down a rigid pattern. It is hoped that they will create a hunger or reveal a need which is not felt at present. These suggestions, or a combination of them, can aid in planning a dignified, significant, worthwhile anniversary for a church.

LEADERSHIP

The official board of the church is the logical steering committee for the anniversary, although a special committee named for this purpose is not out of order. If a special committee is named, it should contain representatives from all age groups, men, women, youth, and from all boards and committees. When all areas of the church work are represented in the committee, decisions can be made, cooperation best maintained, and communication lines to all groups in the church kept open.

A systematic approach is necessary to get things done on time and to have them dovetail into other activities. Certain boards and committees will be challenged with specific responsibilities. All work accomplished and problems to be solved should be reported at frequent meetings of the steering committee.

A representative of each board and committee, and of each participating group, must be present at each of the meetings. When the designated person cannot be present, a responsible substitute should be named to take his place.

Developments should be shared with the whole church body as occasion permits through announcements, bulletins, newsletters, special letters, and telephone calls. When the whole church is kept informed, the anniversary planning and execution will proceed in an orderly and pleasing fashion.

As the time for special events draws near, even more frequent meetings are necessary. Even with the most minute and careful planning, oversights will be discovered which need to be corrected. Moreover, areas will be revealed where a unique facet of an anniversary celebration can be developed. The latter should be seized upon as an opportunity to weave a creative uniqueness into the festive planning.

No one should get upset with the infinite details that seem to be painful trivia in planning a celebration. Everything has a part. As a motorist speeds across the country on superhighways, he gives but little thought to the hours of work that were necessary to build every mile of road. There are mapping, surveying, filling, grading, draining, bridging, surfacing, and erection of directional signs. So it is in these next few pages. Figuratively, they stop to examine the roadbed. The process may seem technical, and even boring, but it will lead to high quality in the finished product. Any part may be questioned or challenged, but the worker's conscientious and joyous best must be built into the whole.

SCHEDULE AND CHECKLIST

The following is a schematic, dated schedule of work to be done during the six months before the anniversary year begins. Each church will adopt part of it, add to it, and reject some of it. Individuals, boards, and committees can use it as a checklist for their accomplishments. The letter "A" is merely an abbreviation for the words "anniversary celebration." Figures refer to months.

A minus 6: Boards and Committees actively brainstorming.
Challenge to plan and prepare.
Official Anniversary Committee selected, and monthly meetings begin.
Decisions on history: author, deadline, cost, financing.

A minus 5: General planning, overall survey.
Physical facilities which need repair, improvement.
Office facilities and staff.
Short-term and long-range goals.

A minus 4: Inquiring of other churches and pastors about their anniversary observances.
Gathering materials and programs.
Beginning chapter by chapter study and report of *Celebrating Your Church Anniversary*.
Challenging boards and committees to accept a month for special emphasis of their own work, or to accept some other responsibility.

A minus 3: Church history report.
Decision on picture directory or yearbook.

A minus 2: Frequent checks and reports on progress.
Reports to congregation, denominational news organs, local papers, TV, radio.
Church history report.
Plans for funding for all or part of the anniversary.

A minus 1: Determining final plans.
Press releases: Include pictures, and any dramatic historic discoveries.
Plans for highlight month, week, or day.
Preparation of special guests and invitation list.
Assignment of schedule and follow-up of invitations.

Space should be provided above to jot in specific and unique anniversary suggestions. These can be a particular joy to a local congregation for they take into account not only the unique history of the specific church but also geographic, ethnic, and social factors which are peculiar to the neighborhood of the church.

Now the anniversary year has arrived. Planning has been going on for many months. Plans have been crystallized and are ready for execution. The following monthly emphases may be changed to suit the individual church. They should not disrupt, but rather aid and highlight the ongoing program of the church.

CHART OF THE YEAR

	Monthly emphases	*Responsibility*
January	Youth	Youth Fellowships Board of Christian Education
February	Mission school of missions missionary speakers	Board of Missions

March	Evangelism preaching, visitation, community involvement, neighborhood meetings	Board of Deacons
April	Sacred music recitals	Music Committee, Choir, Organist
May	Christian education	Board of Christian Education
June	Anniversary banquet exhibits historian's autograph party period dress special speakers	Cabinet or Anniversary Committee
July	Church family picnic	Ad hoc Committee
August	Religious Art	Ad hoc Committee
September	Pageant	Cabinet or Anniversary Committee
October	Local Project	Christian Concern Committee
November	Stewardship	Trustees
December	Church School past and present thoughts for future	Church School Teachers, Board of Christian Education

January	Annual Meeting evaluation and long range plans for a challenge program	Cabinet and Congregation

The following is another checklist that has been found helpful. It contains further details and is organized in a format different from the preceding list. It may provide further stimulation for structuring a detailed observance of an anniversary which is uniquely that of a particular church, and it should be tailored for that purpose. (An analysis of the anniversaries of four churches appears in the Appendix, pages 90-91.) Every celebration should offer Christian witness and appreciation for those who earnestly wrought the history and tradition of a church.

CHECKLIST OF SPECIFICS

Church History	*Pageant*	*Exhibit*
Author	Author	Collector and coordinator
Printing, duplicated, offset, letterpress	Director and Producer	Materials, pictures, awards, programs, news items, etc.
Hard cover or paper	Cast	
Pictures	Production date	Display
Sale or gift	Advertising	Permanent historical file
Other:	Other:	Other:
Monthly Emphases	*Homecoming Week*	*Pin It Down:*
Christian education	Invitations	*Who*
Mission	Banquet	will
Evangelism	Worship and dedication service	do
Stewardship		*what*
Community involvement	Special observances	*when?*
	Art exhibit	
Ecumenical dialogue and action	Recognition of special guests	Report meetings
Other:	Other:	Creative changes:

A circle divided into sectors can provide another view of the detailed planning. This gives a whole view of the anniversary. Sectors may be drawn and filled in according to the group's desires and decisions.

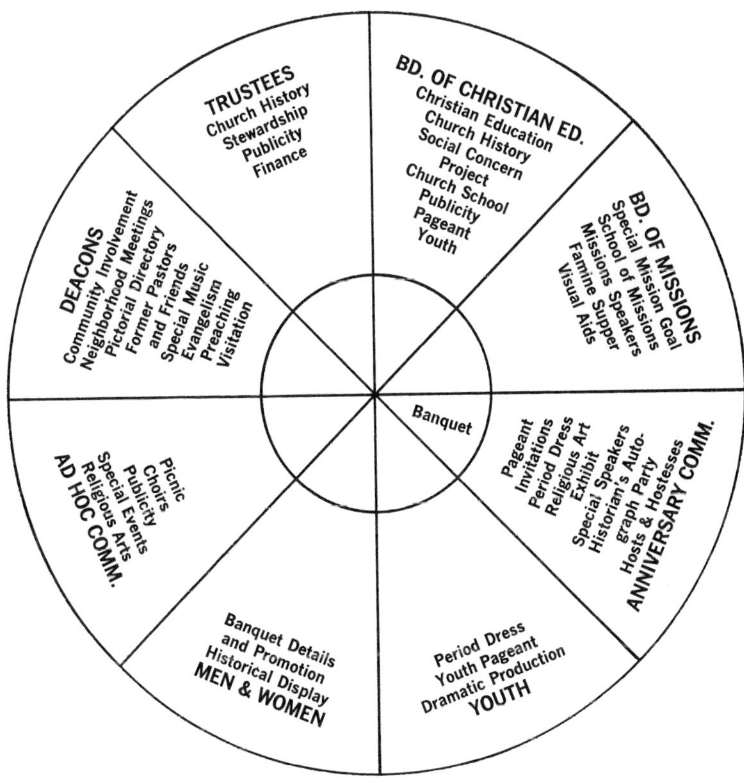

Of course, the foregoing does not exhaust the anatomy of an anniversary. The Greece Baptist Church, near Rochester, New York, has set a scholarly and creative example. The pastor researched and prepared a series of "Faith of Our Fathers" services over the course of the anniversary year. The first twenty-five year period of the church's history was remembered by selecting and repeating a sermon from the pen of Horace Bushnell. Music such as that used in churches at that time was rendered. Next, a sermon that was originally preached by Phillips Brooks highlighted the second twenty-five year period. The third quarter-century was recalled with a sermon by Walter Rauschenbusch. The fourth sermon of the series was chosen by Harry Emerson Fosdick as representative of his preaching in that period of the church's history. Finally, a predecessor who had held the pulpit of the Greece Church for some thirty-eight years preached in person to bring the series up-to-date.

The town was caught up in the spirit of the celebration with the presentation of a drama entitled "From Strength to Strength," which depicted Christian, Baptist, town, and church history. Much of the drama's content came from an anniversary booklet with the same title written by the Reverend J. Ralph Shotwell, who was pastor of the Greece Baptist Church at that time.

During the anniversary year at the First Baptist Church in New Haven, Connecticut, religious leaders were asked to speak to the general theme, "A Faith for Changing Times." Dr. Luther Weigel, Dr. Edwin H. Tuller, Dr. Kenneth Latourette, and Dr. Roland Bainton were invited to speak to the theme. Their addresses, which were preserved on tape, offered wisdom based on unchanging faith, truly a faith for changing times.

6

Telling the Story (Publicity)

Church people need to get excited about the church and its mission. People become enthusiastic about a movie or drama, a new fashion, a new car, or a new hairdo. The "Palm Sunday" aspect of the Christian faith needs to be publicized. Although the "Good Friday" experiences are a part of the church's life, the church must always remember that Easter's joys surmount the dark gloom of Good Friday.

An anniversary provides the opportunity to rejoice in the Christian faith and to bear witness to that faith in a world which often has turned a deaf ear. The message of the church is of the highest importance and quality. It can bring peace and direction to a world which sorely needs them. It can challenge youth, comfort the aged, and look to the future as well as the past. It can lead to intelligent change under the guidance of the Holy Spirit. It can replace boredom with excitement, hate with love, greed with unselfishness, and fear with confidence. It can even replace death with life — abundant life now and eternal life in the future. This is the Christian faith to be proclaimed from antenna tops and space satellites. Christian people have the privilege and the duty to use

every communication medium possible to build the bridge from the merciful and loving God to a world going its own way in confusion.

The anniversary is a time to tell the community, denomination, and interdenominational groups the great good news of Emmanuel – God with the church which seeks to be a healing, comforting, challenging word of God in the world. Here is an opportunity to tell of the hopes and dreams of the past and present generations.

Newspaper and denominational publications are interested. They offer the opportunity to tell the unchurched in the community what the church stands for, what it is trying to do, what resources it calls upon, and what help it needs to accomplish its task. Other denominations are interested in unique and effective expressions which may develop in the anniversary celebration of a church.

The leaders of the anniversary celebration should talk over the developing plans with denominational officials and ask for their help and suggestions for statewide and nationwide publicity. Their help can be of a very practical nature in space-allotment in the denominational news media and also with suggestions from other church anniversaries throughout the area. Techniques for picture-taking, stories, and anecdotes will be gladly shared and a good working cooperation established which will be beneficial to the local and statewide work.

Newspaper, radio, and television people may be consulted about the problem of sharing the story of the local church and its history. They will be found to be most interested, and often they are dedicated people themselves with deep religious interests. They will become enthusiastic about the story of the church. They will be glad to advise, make suggestions, and generally put their facilities to work along with those of the local church in telling the story. They know the language and the idiom of the day and can translate the religious purpose of the church into dramatic and interesting terms. Interviews can be arranged for special speakers and highlights of the celebrations picked up for state and area coverage. In some cases national television will pick up a particularly dramatic event, as they did when the pastor in Haverhill, Massachusetts, arrived at a two hundredth anniversary celebration in colonial dress and on horseback.

The warning of one newspaper man to a pastor of a local church needs to be heeded. He reminded the pastor, who had been complaining about the lack of communication between the church and the public, that the church was not advertising a circus. There has to be a dignity which is inherent in the "product" which the church is advertising. Communication of the circus variety would defeat the whole purpose of the church. Nevertheless, the story of the church can be told with taste and effectiveness. It can contain dignity but also the urgency, variety, and excitement which are part of the Christian faith.

The church ofttimes becomes shoddy and careless in its communication. News bulletins and plans are shared only with an "in" group who have become accustomed to ecclesiastical lingo while the uninitiated public is left completely uninformed. The holier-than-thou attitude expressed in artificial, ministerial tones must be dropped if communication to the minds and needs of the world is to be effected. Someone has pointed out that Christ was sent for the world, not expressly for "St. John's by the Gas Station." The fundamental good news, which must be told in every possible manner, is that God through Christ has the power of redemption for the world. Anniversary events are opportunities to bring this good news to the grass roots level.

An anniversary presents an occasion to tune up the whole church and to present its image to the public. Certainly, any telling of the story would reveal the deep meaning of the church's worship, evangelism, stewardship, mission, and meaning for the civilization of which it is a part. This should be done in a variety of ways and at various and frequent times during the anniversary year. All the regular avenues of communication and publicity can be utilized, including pulpit announcements, news bulletins, bulletin boards, announcements in societies, committees, and boards, and even a poster contest for the youth of the church.

Pictures, snapshots, portraits, slides, and even moving pictures can be used at different functions of the anniversary celebration. It would be well to have someone designated as the official photographer, though others also might be encouraged to bring their equipment. On occasion, the local newspaper photographer or the TV cameras can be invited for some newsworthy event. The official church photographer should think in terms of glossy prints which could be used for newspapers or denominational publications. The polaroid camera is a quick way to get a picture for a halftone cut or for use in offset printing.

Along with pictures go sounds. Tape recordings of special addresses, musical programs, or a play or pageant are lasting links with the past and the future. Today, the means are available for recording history in at least three dimensions – the printed word, the recorded word of sound, and the photograph. These record the reality of today in a way which will become more and more valuable as the years go by. They are a stimulating testimony to and documentary evidence of a fellowship in the very act and sound of being a fellowship.

An outstanding example of the way in which pictures can be used to tell the story is the job done by Central Baptist Church of Hartford, Connecticut, on its one hundred seventy-fifth anniversary. Seven historical panels were painted in vivid colors depicting the surge of history, local and world-wide, and somewhere in each panel the church is embodied, seemingly like a spiritual Rock of Gibraltar. The artist was the Reverend J. Thomas Leamon. Before his ordination, Mr. Leamon was a professional artist, a graduate of Rhode Island School of Design in Providence, and an illustrator for texts, periodicals, and trade novels.

These panels catch up the seven periods of the church's history and are a permanent pictorial record. They have been reproduced in black and white in an anniversary booklet which contains an historical survey and a special scholarly script prepared from original sources by Doris Brinker, Director of Christian Education at Central Baptist Church. The unique scanning and prosodic structure of the verse add to the beauty and clarity of the script.

Part V of this series is the 1927 to 1947 era. The emphasis in this is the great depression and the ministry of the church to the victims of economic distress. The ticker-tape reader has his back to the church, and emphasizes the separation of business and Christianity. Continuing in this atmosphere of competition, the flapper and the garish movie marquee come in front of the church building. In the upper right, a new era beclouds the scene with the mushrooming atom bomb. In the upper left is Judson Tower at the American Baptist Assembly, Green Lake, Wisconsin, and just below is the portrait of Dr. J. Melvin Prior, the church's dynamic pastor from 1942 to 1947.

Below is a practical checklist to help get good publicity. The Anniversary Committee can brainstorm even more and come up with further suggestions to fit the particular situation and story of the local church.

Pulpit announcements
Newsletters and Sunday bulletins
Bulletin boards
A youth poster contest
Newspaper stories at regular intervals
Spot announcements on TV and/or radio
Denominational papers and news bulletins
Pictures to papers and denominational news media with brief captions
Anecdotes from history
Coupling of anniversary announcements with news stories of the ongoing life of the church
Notification to papers and TV about approaching events, including when, where, and why. (Go over the schedule of events with editors.)
Pictures and stories for special speakers and programs
General outline for a news highlight each month
Interviews of speakers by newspaper and TV reporters
Letterhead with founding date and date of anniversary
Rubber stamp for letters
Anniversary coin in silver or bronze
Invitations to denominational officials to all functions
Invitations to radio, TV, and newspaper reporters to all events (Make these personal invitations, not only with an eye to the publicity which might be forthcoming, but to build goodwill for future

stories whether or not the reporters publish an account of the particular event.)

In addition to these items, a "Checklist for a Historical Inventory of a Local Church," prepared by Professor Ford L. Battles and the Reverend Arthur E. Wilson, has been included in the Appendix of this book. This checklist shows the scope and depth necessary in the accumulation of data for the present anniversary and the future historian.

The time has come to cast aside the caution engendered by years of criticism, discounting, deriding, and despairing from both within and without the church. The institutional church has been a target for criticism for years. Through an anniversary celebration, a local church can turn the tide. Its members can celebrate and shout the ideals which are the living core of the church of Christ. These ideals provide ever new ways for renewal and new life in each succeeding generation.

7

Further Program Suggestions

No one should feel overwhelmed by the number of suggestions already given and the impossibility of carrying out even a few of them. Let it be repeated, no church can or should attempt to use all of the suggestions. The long list and the great variety have been given to stimulate local creativity and expression and to involve everyone and all groups in the celebration activities. In addition, some of these suggestions may be used to enrich a church's program during the years following the anniversary year, thus raising the church's ministry to a higher plateau of effectiveness and aliveness. An anniversary is a shuttle activating a process for church renewal that can be woven into the fabric of the church history.

The vision of the Morgan Park Baptist Church, Chicago, Illinois, provides an example. This church took a mortgage of $25,000 on its buildings to aid the Mexico Baptist Seminary in Mexico City. Although this was done as a part of their regular program and not in connection with an anniversary, it is an idea that could be used by any church as a part of its anniversary celebration. A church could begin by mortgaging its assets to start a new work in another area of its own city or town, or to make a thrust into a mission area. What better way could there be to recapture the daring of the founders of the church! What better step of faith could there be! What better assessment of the strength and weakness of a fellowship, and what a renewed sense that all depends upon the grace and the blessing of the Lord!

One pastor remarked that in each generation something new comes to the churches as a means of expressing themselves and communicating their message to each other and to the community. The something new for this generation, he thought, was the production of a yearbook containing the pictures of church members and their families, a message from the pastor, possibly the Lord's Prayer or other devotional thought, and additional pages that summarize the highlights of the history of the church. The sittings for the family portraits were made at the church, but the families were under no pressure to buy pictures when they saw the proofs. In any case, the company that made the pictures produced the booklet and provided, free of charge, sufficient copies for the membership of the church. The book was a tremendous help to the fellowship of the church. Persons who had been politely speaking to each other for years were able to attach a name to each face. The nominating or personnel committee had an easier time because they could identify in the directory the persons being considered for office. Also, it was a pictorial prayer book, enabling individuals to pray for the members of the church more readily and specifically by means of the visual aid of the family portraits.

ADDITIONAL PROGRAM SUGGESTIONS

Hold lecture series
Hold organ and musical recitals
Prepare an anniversary hymn, both words and music
Recognize former pastors
Recognize church members entering full-time church-related vocations

Recognize special Christian service
Order anniversary favors, such as a book, awards, a plate, or a medal
Give copies of church history to strategic libraries and seminaries
Tape record and film special events and addresses
Honor members of long standing; such as 25 and 50 years
Have couple attend anniversary service in period dress. (Use transportation of the period, such as horse and surrey)
Exhibit earliest horseless carriage beside the church

Revisit sites of former buildings
Sponsor refugee family or families
Send special gifts and greetings to missionaries
Prepare anniversary picture directory of families and leading boards and committees
Appoint an historian to summarize highlights of each church year at annual meeting
Prepare time capsule for another generation
See immediate goals and long-range goals
Publicize anniversary events in newspapers, denominational publications, and wherever possible

The space below is set aside for notes on possible programs and projects for the local church. The thinking of many persons on the anniversary committee will enable the meetings of the group to produce tangible results. After individual views and hopes have been expressed and discussed, the group thinking can come to the surface. As the members of the church work together to achieve a satisfactory goal, a rich, new fellowship develops. Herein lies much of the joy of an anniversary.

8

History and Pageant

What are some practical suggestions about researching and writing the history or getting the materials needed as background for a pageant or still life presentation? Writing with authority on this phase of the anniversary is Dr. John W. Brush, Professor of Church History, Emeritus, Andover Newton Theological School, who has written a number of historical accounts of churches. Dr. Brush also wrote the pageant for the one hundred twenty-fifth anniversary celebration of the Connecticut Baptist Convention.

HISTORY

Recently, Dr. Brush shared some of the accumulated wisdom from these experiences in a small article entitled "Writing Histories of Three New England Churches."[1] He says:

"Vitality, color, and sparkle are needed in historical writing. There is much to do to disabuse a host of Americans of their distaste for history. If they could only see that history is people, is persons, is life! In its place, the date of the great event is important, but the historian should make one see the flash of the hero's eyes, and make one hear the ring of his voice. The researcher must indeed drag his feet through heaps of statistics. Treasurers' and clerks' reports can be dull indeed. Yet further research, as into the memories of those who are contemporaries and into the yellowing pages of letters, may bring forth the colorful detail that illuminates the narrative and entrances the reader. In one of the histories featured in this article, it was the newspaper's dramatic headlining of a certain crisis in the church that brightened a whole page for the reader.

"A chance conversation with a friend gave the writer the kind of detail he rejoiced to find, and he recorded thus: 'A member who recalls the days of the uniting of the churches, tells us of the drum-beat of the children's feet on the wooden blocks of Warren Avenue's pavement, as the entire Church School paraded over to Back Bay to realize formal union with the scholars of First Baptist.'

"Let the historian learn to hear the history in the rhythmic beat of the March of the men of faith, following Christ Our Captain."

Dr. Brush also suggests that church histories need a backdrop larger than the local scene. He writes:

"Such volumes of local church history may be of use to the research historian, and attract local readers of an antiquarian bent. Their pages tend to be, to the general or average reader, dry as powder, so heavily laden with statistics, names, dates, genealogies, and myriad unrelated items. They often fail to relate the reader to the larger scene: The nation's life, the world's crying problems, the thought-patterns of the passing generations."

Memories of colorful incidents may distort the facts. Consequently, recollections should always be supplemented by the written records. A humorous incident illustrating this is shared by Dr. Brush who courageously deflates his own ego in the telling of it:

"Here is an instance of the author's own mistakes. About

twenty-five years previously, he had preached in the Haverhill church. It was a bitter cold Sunday evening, really bitter cold. Memories of that service made him want to record them, for first-hand materials add color and vitality. On that occasion the church had been almost completely filled, meaning nearly a thousand in attendance. Thus it was recorded in the manuscript. Today's pastor, C. C. Meeden, thought to look into the very complete records in the church office, and there discovered there had been only 323 in attendance that evening. Touché!"

However, in a book review of Brush's *History of First Baptist Church in New Haven — 1816-1966,* Dr. Roland H. Bainton, of Yale University, gives assurance that Brush, his former pupil, was authentic in his background research and writing. He wrote:

"The story of the First Baptist Church in New Haven by John Brush covers the enormous span of her antecedents and history in brief and readable compass. All of the major phases of American church life are touched upon in his pages." And again, "This booklet will be of interest to a wider public because this congregation is set in the framework of New England church life." [2]

A final note about length and indication of some of the internal struggle and work that goes into each volume of church history, however small, is found in this comment by Dr. Brush (in the work previously cited):

"Histories of two or three hundred pages would have demanded much more time and labor. Yet without painstaking and time-consuming work, it would have been impossible to put even these briefer books together. This is, of course, the nature of history-writing. The stacks of notes for these histories look very bulky alongside the slender bound volumes. Boiling down, organizing, then the writing and re-writing — thus the big shapeless mass was transformed into a trim little book. Yet there had been another step — the reading, correcting and the suggesting on the part of a committee of readers in each case. Some definite mistakes and omissions were thus revealed. Some obvious gaps were filled. Yet in some few cases the author had to insist, as against certain preferred corrections, on his own rightness."

The local church historian will find a great deal of help in the task of collecting and organizing historical material in the "Checklist for a Historical Inventory of a Local Church" which has been included in the Appendix of this book.

PAGEANT

The church is not in competition with the commercial theater but nevertheless it may legitimately try to communicate by means of drama. Indeed, the drama began as a religious rite and was a medium of worship. A pageant is a re-enactment of the past which projects truths to the present.

The hour or so that it takes to present a pageant reviewing the history of a local church is not the end in view. The total production beginning with the search for documents for the history, and continuing through the making of an orderly arrangement, the selection of highlights, the writing of the script, the staging, selection of actors, and the rehearsals—all of these build up a fellowship among those who would communicate their sense of the leading of Christ in the church's history.

The pageant, *Called to Freedom,* a dramatization of three hundred years of history of The First Baptist Church of Boston, was written by the pastor, Charles W. Griffin. The background history was taken from *A History of First Baptist Church of Boston* by Nathan Wood, 1899, and *Legacy of Faith* by John W. Brush, 1965. The pageant was later revised and presented to the Massachusetts Baptist Convention. The narrators were professionally trained. All others participated in the tableaux only. There were no speaking parts. The tableaux were set within a large frame forty by fifteen feet, covered by a "scrim," a cheesecloth type of screen. When the scrim was lighted from the balconies, scenes could be changed without the audience detecting any movement. As the spotlights from the balconies went out, stage lights went on behind the scrim, revealing the tableaux through the transparent covering.

Another pageant, *Appointment with History, 125 Years of the Connecticut Baptist Convention,* was written by John W. Brush. Although one would expect instructions for the stage setting to be quite dull, excitement does mount, and anticipation is whetted. The past is about to come alive. Because of the number of participants, one can imagine the fellowship as they prepared in rehearsals for the presentation.

APPOINTMENT WITH HISTORY: 125 YEARS OF THE CONNECTICUT BAPTIST CONVENTION

The chancel contains the choir which has an important part in the evening's work; and the mid-chancel has twelve small chairs arranged about a small table.

In the pew-section, various groups are seated as the director determines. Of these most important is a group of thirty-eight men, the founders of the convention in 1823. These may be in costume or not as the director chooses.

There are groups of about twenty each of pastors, laymen, women, young people, and ethnic groups of about twenty each (men and women) of Germans, Swedes, Italians, and Negroes. Sound effects come from a drummer and a group of ten voices offstage.

Instructions emphasize the need for an excellent reader as so much depends upon him. There is a scant minimum of pictorial, symbolic, and dramatic effects, so good timing and good voicing must keep the pageant moving and alive.

Then comes the organ prelude, something with the dignity of Handel's *Largo*. As the music fades, the lights brighten.

Reader: Baptists of Connecticut, this night you have an appointment with history. Just for this hour, forget the rush and the gallop of time outside these walls. Let us fortify our spirits with the recollection of a company of those called Baptist who have served the Lord Christ and labored in His Kingdom in this our well-loved state. Our state! Silvered down the middle by a lordly river; washed along its whole southern front by a broad arm of the sea; embraced on three sides by sister-states of power and renown; our Connecticut boasts a history potent to rouse men and women to new faith and hope and action. Over these rolling miles of wooded hills and green fields, the pioneers of three centuries ago built their farms and villages, and lifted the walls of their temples. The unanimous verdict of history is that they built well. Their children and their children's children have wrought continuing good. Tonight we honor our forefathers in the faith, and ask God for the will and the grace to follow on where they began. . . ."

9

Summary and Sampling of Anniversaries

The six areas of activity suggested in Chapter 2 will provide a foundation upon which a valid anniversary celebration can be built. This foundation guarantees that the celebration will be a fitting expression of appreciation for the past and at the same time a preparation for the work of the present and the future.

This chapter will help the church to build a superstructure on this foundation. Anniversary celebrations are vastly different from each other. Some make use of one combination of ingredients to form their superstructures and others make use of other combinations. The foundation and superstructure together must result in a celebration that is particularly significant for a specific church at a specific time.

The point is that an anniversary is not an attempt to strive after novelty, nor is it ever merely a mimic of another celebration. While it is being thoughtfully planned according to the stated principles, the creative aspects of an anniversary should be explored, and if something different, novel, and having variety comes forth, so much the better.

This chapter is in the nature of a survey. It is geographically extensive and reaches beyond the personal experience of the pastors and executive ministers to whom it was sent. Replies were returned in greater numbers than expected. Also personal interviews with pastors, priests, and laymen helped to round out the information about anniversaries and how they are celebrated in Protestant and Catholic churches in the United States and Canada.

A simple letter of inquiry was sent out. The basic outline of the anniversary event was solicited. The general impression, the usefulness of anniversaries, and the how and why of observing them were elicited in the replies, often accompanied with personal letters and memorabilia. We hope this information can help stimulate the further gathering of facts and experiences. Here is the letter:

> Dear Colleague:
>
> Greetings! I hope this isn't the straw which breaks your patience. Please find a minute or two to write a word about any church anniversary you have experienced. Personally I have had four, one in each of my four pastorates, and each proved to be a source of vigor and renewal. I am gathering material for a resource book on church anniversaries.
>
> I'd be grateful to you if you will fill in below.
>
> 1. Church history written? Published? Cost?
> 2. Pageant prepared and produced?
> 3. Historical display?
> 4. Period dress evening?
> 5. Any unique feature or features of your anniversary?
> 6. Other?
> 7. Evaluation and changes you would make from wisdom of hindsight?
>
> Many thanks and cordially,
> Alvin D. Johnson
>
> P.S., Any anniversary bulletins or memorabilia you might share with me will be safely returned to you.

Although this survey was not exhaustive, it proved to be an excellent sampling of the attitudes, the responses, and the accomplishments of anniversaries.

The pastor of The First Congregational Church of Berkeley, California wrote: "Yes, we did have a good time with the church anniversary both in Middletown and in Waterbury (Conn.). Each celebration was connected with a capital funds drive. It seemed to be a good time for raising money to refurbish the buildings. In Waterbury we put on an elaborate pageant and published a book."

Another reply stated, "Former pastors welcomed back with *five* attending."

One former pastor wrote of his inability to attend an anniversary, but by means of a taped greeting accompanied by photos, he and his wife had a part in the festivities.

At the one hundred twenty-fifth anniversary of a state

convention an elaborate historical pageant was written by Dr. John W. Brush, then Professor at Andover Newton Theological School, and presented by a cast of 100 persons under the skilled direction of Amy Goodhue Loomis.

One reply from the Pacific Northwest shared the view that "the churches of the West do not do nearly as much as the churches of the East do relative to anniversaries." When they are older, perhaps they will.

A reply from an executive minister from Oregon: "My observation is that the best commemorations of significant anniversaries, as 50th, 75th, or centennial, come from utilizing all the above you have mentioned with something of each scattered throughout the year — with some observance each month."

One small church integrated special cottage prayer meetings, the weekly prayer service, and the Sunday morning services around the two meditation-discussion topics, "What could our church do if we had more faith?" and "How can we get this kind of faith?" This just preceded an anniversary week with special speakers and a banquet.

Colorado mentioned a seventy-fifth anniversary booklet (pictures and history of each church) costing $4,000.00, and a pageant presented by the drama department of Colorado's Woman's College (now Temple Buell College).

Replies revealed an anniversary hymn and/or poem is not uncommon, and its creation depends upon the talents of some member of the church.

In a western church, a Colorado carnation was given to each person present. A different color was used for each ten-year span of membership.

One pastor and church are working on a new constitution which they hope will be adopted on the two hundred thirtieth anniversary of the church.

Several churches have had picture directories made in connection with anniversary celebrations. In one instance, several additional pages were purchased from the photographic company and used to publish a revised history of the church. Because of the family sittings (no pressure to buy) the book cost the church nothing. This was an economical way to have the history printed and distributed.

One church with a seventy-fifth anniversary in its background is looking forward to an eightieth celebration which will be directed more to the community than to the church members.

One pastor, writing of a recent one hundredth anniversary, concluded: "Excellent results, with involvement of large number of people."

Iowa had its religious history dramatized in two pageants, *People of Vision,* and *Centennial Pageant.* The latter was presented at Red Oak, Iowa, to about 1,200 people. There were 84 in the cast and 150 in the choir. In Montgomery County a centennial celebration rallied some 7,000 people to hear an address by E. Stanley Jones. There were 300 in the choir. A continuing result is that a county religious rally is held every year on the Sunday night before the fair, which opens on Monday.

When the oldest Protestant church in New Mexico recently celebrated its centennial, Governor David Cargo participated in the dedication of a plaque marking the anniversary. This church, the First Presbyterian Church of Santa Fe, was organized by the Reverend David F. McFarland on January 6, 1867. He arrived in November, 1866, by stagecoach over the Santa Fe Trail with a commission from the Board of Domestic Missions of the Presbyterian Church. After holding services on the first Sunday, he organized a day school within a week. The need for a full-time teacher attracted the attention of church women in Auburn, New York, who organized the "Santa Fe Association" to aid the mission in the southwest.

The original twelve members of the church included an ecumenical congregation of three Presbyterians, two Lutherans, and three members of the Christian Church.

After the manner of many church records which contain unusual facts, this church has the unique distinction of recording the marriage of the mother of the western outlaw Billy the Kid to her second husband. Billy was in church on that occasion as one of the witnesses.

At the Clough Centenary Celebration held in Ongole, South India, September 14-18, 1966, there were song services, Bible readings, and prayers. Sermons could be heard morning, afternoon, and evening as the people gathered to fulfill the theme: "Zeal for the Glory of God." State dignitaries, the granddaughter of John E. Clough, Mrs. Gladys Clough Rowland, and her daughter — Clough's great-granddaughter — along with hospital leaders, representatives of American Baptists, evangelists from the Billy Graham team, and the pastor of the Jewett Memorial Church, who had just returned from a year's study at Colgate Rochester Divinity School, joined in the 100th anniversary festivities. The meetings came to a close with a sunrise service on Prayer Meeting Hill at 6 A.M. and a morning worship at 9:00 A.M. The spirit of thanksgiving was caught up in the Scripture text: "Thanks be to God, who giveth us the victory through our Lord Jesus Christ. Wherefore, my beloved brethren, be ye stedfast, unmoveable, always abounding in the work of the Lord, forasmuch as ye know that your labor is not in vain in the Lord" (1 Corinthians 15:57-58, ASV).

And a fervent hope was caught up in the text: "Now unto him that is able to do exceeding abundantly above all that we ask or think, according to the power that worketh in us, unto him be the glory in the church and in Christ Jesus unto all generations for ever and ever. Amen" (Ephesians 3:20-21, ASV).

An American church that was celebrating its one hundred fiftieth anniversary had the privilege of sharing a treasured old communion service with Christian brothers who were rejoicing in 100 years of Christian life and witness in their church in Ongole, India.

How are church anniversaries celebrated in Canada, especially in the Maritimes? The Reverend Carolyn Palmer, who has worked and observed extensively throughout the region, notes that in general the anniversary celebration seems more a setting for sociability and appreciation of the past and present than a production.

First, a Roll Call Service is one type of celebration which may be held in a small or rural church. The service includes special music, special speaker, and the calling of the church roll by the church clerk. Each person present responds to his name with a verse of Scripture. Those who are from a distance or are unable to attend usually send a letter of greeting and a special offering.

At the anniversary time many small churches try to contact non-resident members in an effort to keep ties with them or to encourage them to move their membership to another church where they live.

A fellowship hour often follows the service. This is a time when old friends meet. People who have been away come home for the occasion, and usually visitors from neighboring communities come for the service.

Second, a Church Birthday and Birthday Party may be used by the good-sized town church each year. The regular morning service includes special music and a guest speaker. The evening service is a communion service. Again, as in the rural churches, there is a fellowship hour. During the hour such things as a quiz on the history of the church, a poem written especially for the occasion, or an historical drama or pageant relives and refreshes the significance of the past. Elderly members of the congregation are usually honored in some way for their contribution. They are given special citation or special mention.

Refreshments include a specially decorated birthday cake for the church. The honor of making the first cut is often given to the person who has been a church member the longest.

Thus the ties and the obligations of the past are renewed. New courage and determination are summoned forth for the present and for the task which lies ahead. Appreciation for the total life of the church of Christ and for his work is enhanced, and a sense of the vital link which the present provides with a colorful past and an exciting future is highlighted with gratitude and renewed endeavor and resolution.

Are anniversaries always successful? No, they do not always reach the goals which are set for them. On one occasion there was a small attendance at the beginning of one week's anniversary program even though the publicity and buildup seemed to be adequate and the speaker was an outstanding denominational leader. One solution to such a problem is to involve as many people as possible in some meaningful activity of the celebration.

Sometimes circumstances upset the most carefully laid plans of men. Take, for example, the Centennial Celebration of Brazil's Methodists planned for August of 1967. Eula Kennedy Long, writing from Sao Paulo, Brazil, begins *The Christian Century* article, "Unfortunately, what had been planned as an enthusiastic celebration August 6-7 of Methodism's 100th birthday in Brazil proved to be, in common parlance, a 'flop.'" The article lists reasons for the failure, and these could well be the booby traps which could wreck any celebration.

"There were several reasons for the failure: lack of agreement on whether the founding date was 1876 or 1867; decision on 1867 too late for effective publicity, planning and carry-through in a country where postal and wire communications are still slow and unreliable; gloom created by the split in the church . . . and the fact that the withdrawal of six pastors and some 700 members occurred in the First region (conference), where the big convocation was to be held; disappointment because Martin Luther King, Jr. turned down the invitation to be the main speaker — and too late for the planners to schedule a replacement who would attract not only Brazilian Methodists but other Brazilians." [3]

Gaius Glenn Atkins, in a little pamphlet, *The Anniversary of Your Church,* urges local churches to make more of their anniversaries. He writes, "The headlines of history have their day and cease to be, the fellowships of faith, of prayer, praise and worship are of the enduring. . . . In the recapitulation of what a church has done during the years, it writes a chapter both to be treasured and continued. The real history of a community is oftener in the records of its church than in its official annals. . . .

"It is wise, therefore, that all our churches be reminded of the significance of their own histories, the invaluable quality of their records, and the care that these be faithfully kept. . . . In their own lengthening pasts, still living, the churches grow always more abundant in grace and goodness, and through the witness of the love and care of God abundantly vouchsafed them, they can face their future with clearer vision, unafraid." [4]

This resource book has been prepared for a do-it-yourself leader, committee, or church. A unique, creative job of facing up to the potentialities and possibilities of an anniversary celebration is squarely before the reader. Here is the chance to release fresh ideas and imagination. Here is the chance to get a new focus on the Christian work which is being done in the present. Here is the chance to muster enthusiasm and courage for the thrust into the future. Here is the chance for the renewal of the church where renewal is needed at the grass-roots level.

As the anniversary theme is pursued, by-products can accrue to the church. The structure and functioning of groups, the motivating of the inner dynamics, the moving of a democratic group to new and challenging goals are not lost when the anniversary year has come to a close. These persist as evidence of a hidden strength ready to be called into action whenever the church dedicates itself to assessment and evaluation against the standard of the Spirit of the living, moving Christ. When, with new clarity, the church group realizes the motivating spirit of the Christ in past accomplishments, or sees the reason for failures because of unattainable goals or lack of unity, there is a fresh allegiance to the Head of the church and a more consuming desire to make his will their own.

10

Religious Observance and Dedication

In all the activity of the anniversary celebration which may be extended over a whole year, or concentrated in a month or a week, the central meaning of the anniversary should be caught up in the religious observance of the event by such activities as special prayers, religious services, and specially prepared home altar devotions. An anniversary is a pilgrimage back to the source of strength and direction.

History, pageant, fund raising, period dress, liturgical art, pictorial directory, social events, special programs — all these have their place in the anniversary year. But the central elements of the anniversary are thanksgiving for the leadership of God over the years and gratitude to those who have gone before and who listened to the voice of God, those who counted it a privilege to sacrifice that the Word of the Lord might be heard, taught, and felt in merciful healing.

A service of prayer and thanksgiving is the heart of the celebration. It catches up gratitude and resolution for commitment for the present and future. It is the giving of self even as Isaiah gave himself when he responded in the Temple and said, "Here am I, Lord, send me."

In the spirit of the significance of the devotional nature of an anniversary, some worship materials are offered in this chapter. The following is an anniversary litany of thanks and dedication.

AN ANNIVERSARY LITANY OF THANKS AND DEDICATION

LEADER: O give thanks unto the Lord, for he is our God and there is none beside him. He is our creator, our redeemer, our strength, and our guide.
PEOPLE: We thank thee, O Lord our God. We praise thee with a whole heart.
LEADER: Give thanks unto the Lord our God, for he was in Christ reconciling the world unto himself, and he has entrusted to us the ministry of reconciliation.
PEOPLE: We thank thee, O Lord, our God. We praise thee with a whole heart.
LEADER: Give thanks unto the Lord our God, for he has endowed us with many and various gifts. He has called us to many and various forms of work; but all of them, in all men, are the work of the same God.
PEOPLE: We thank thee, O Lord, our God. We praise thee with a whole heart. Lord, we have heard thy call. We dedicate ourselves anew to follow thy leading.
LEADER AND PEOPLE PRAY TOGETHER:
Our Father and our God, in whom we live and move and have our being, we have heard thy voice calling us to be disciples and to make disciples. We confess that we have not always obeyed these commands, that we have turned to our own way. Forgive us, Lord.

Tonight we come to thee humbly praying. Create clean hearts in us again, O God. Renew right spirits within us. Fill us with the power of thy Spirit, so that we may indeed fulfill the great mission which thou hast entrusted to us.

We do now offer our very selves to thee as living sacrifices. We promise to serve thee according to the gifts given to each of us. So together, as one body in Christ, we shall make all nations thy disciples. In faith we go forth, through Jesus Christ our Lord. Amen.

Morgan Phelps Noyes has the following prayer, "The Anniversary of a Church," in his book *Prayers for Services:*

"Eternal God, our dwelling place in all generations, under

whose guidance our fathers walked, by whom they were strengthened and sustained, and in whom they found the life eternal, we pray that the spirit which kindled their faith may descend upon us this day. We thank thee for every memory which this day revives, and for the cloud of witnesses who make this day sacred for us, and bid us lay aside our sins, looking to him who is the Author and Finisher of faith. Deepen within us the sense of gratitude for sacrifices made for us by those who have gone the way of life before us, and found thy house a place of refreshment and strength. Give us to see by faith the needs of those who shall come after us, and to bequeath to them, as a rich heritage of the spirit, our witness in life and deed to the unsearchable riches of the life with thee. Lead us into a deeper experience of that life, that we may become forerunners of the glorious day when our world shall be the kingdom of our Lord and of his Christ. Amen."[5]

Here is an especially good prayer for an anniversary, written by Walter Rauschenbusch prior to 1909. It is as fresh and challenging today as when he wrote it.

"O God, we pray for thy Church, which is set today amid the perplexities of a changing order, and face to face with a great new task. . . . Oh, Baptize her afresh with the life-giving spirit of Jesus! Grant her a new birth, though it be with the travail of repentance and humiliation. Bestow upon her a more imperious responsiveness to duty, a swifter compassion with suffering, and an utter loyalty to the will of God. Put upon her lips the ancient gospel of her Lord. Help her to proclaim boldly the coming of the Kingdom of God and the doom of all that resist it. Fill her with the prophets' scorn of tyranny, and with a Christlike tenderness for the heavy-laden and down-trodden. Give her faith to espouse the cause of the people, and in their hands that grope after freedom and light to recognize the bleeding hands of the Christ. Bid her cease from seeking her own life, lest she lose it. Make her valiant to give up her life to humanity, that like her crucified Lord she may mount by the path of the cross to a higher glory. Amen." [6]

Here is an anniversary prayer by Dr. C. Elroy Shikles offered on the occasion of the Centennial of the First Baptist Church, Denver, Colorado.

"Our God, as we look back upon spiritual ancestors with thankfulness for their fidelity and love for Thee, we pray that generations yet to come will be thankful that we, too, were faithful in our day.

"Endue thy Church with power so that we, thy servants, may meet effectively the urgent needs of this generation. Enable us to be in flesh and blood and spirit, the extension of our Savior who preached the gospel, healed the brokenhearted, set at liberty the enslaved, and proclaimed the acceptable year of the Lord. . . .

"So long Thy power hath blessed us, sure it still will lead us on. Amen."

This beautiful prayer by Samuel H. Miller in *Prayers for Daily Use* is under the chapter heading of "The Church." It admirably catches up the anniversary spirit and aspirations.

"Under the arches of the years we pray to thee, O God, and seek thy blessing as did our fathers before us. We thank thee for the men who founded this church in their faith; for all who have entered it devoutly and with prayer; for all whose humble labors have cherished it against time's slow ruin; for all whose spiritual agonies have hallowed it; for all who consecrated the joys of earth in its quiet silence and reverent song; for all who kept fellowship with Jesus, meekly and with inner rejoicing. Make us faithful in all things by thy grace that both this sanctuary and our souls may be a light in which men shall see thee and glorify thy name. Amen." [7]

The following list of Scripture references is intended to be appropriate for the worship services connected with anniversary celebrations. Some of these have been chosen from anniversary services, both Catholic and Protestant. Selections may be made from this list for a particular service.

Old Testament
Genesis 1 (selections)
Genesis 9:8-17
Exodus 3 (selections)
Exodus 14 (selections)
Exodus 20 (selections)
Deuternomy 31:7 ff.
Psalms 1; 8; 19; 23; 33; 34; 37:1-18; 89 (selections); 90; 91; 93; 100; 103; 118; 121; 122; 133; 136 (as Litany); 139; 150
Ecclesiastes 12
Isaiah 6:1-8; 40:1-8; 53; 55
Jeremiah 6:16-30

New Testament
Matthew 5:1-16; 18:1-14
John 3:1-16; 15:1-17
Acts 2:1-21
Romans 12
Romans 8:28-39
1 Corinthians 13
2 Corinthians 4
Ephesians 4
Philippians 4 (selections)
James 2:14-26
1 Peter 2:1-10
Revelation 21:1-4

Also use selected responsive readings from the hymnbook.

The Church Covenant is also an important part of the anniversary celebration.

Many hymns reflect the spirit of worship, praise, and thanksgiving to God inherent in an anniversary service. The following is a small list of appropriate hymns. This list is but indicative of many hymns which can catch up the aspirations of the people and express their gratitude. Local taste and familiarity will help to direct the choice of hymns appropriate for the ceremonies.

The Church's One Foundation
God of Grace and God of Glory
Faith of Our Fathers
Rise Up, O Men of God
Blest Be the Tie that Binds
God Send Us Men
Forward Through the Ages
Lead On, O King Eternal
We've a Story to Tell to the Nations
In Christ There Is No East or West
Send Down Thy Truth, O Lord
A Mighty Fortress Is Our God
Light of the World, We Hail Thee
O Worship the King
The Voice of God Is Calling
Great Is Thy Faithfulness
Now Thank We All Our God
How Firm a Foundation
God of Our Fathers, Known of Old
Once to Every Man and Nation
God of Our Fathers; Whose Almighty Hand

The Lord Is My Shepherd
O Zion, Haste, Thy Mission
High Fulfilling
Christ for the World We Sing
I Love to Tell the Story

An outstanding example of an anniversary worship service was held in October, 1967, when all the Lutheran churches in the New Haven, Connecticut, area gathered in Trinity Lutheran Church to worship and celebrate their common inheritance. In two Sunday morning services they observed the four hundred fiftieth anniversary of Martin Luther's courageous act of nailing the ninety-five theses to the church door in Wittenberg, Germany. The Lutheran pastors produced a recording in honor of the anniversary and included music closely associated with the life of Luther and selections from some of his sermons. The title of the record is "Lutheran Legacy."

A newspaper story of the celebration describes the new and creative ways in which the Lutheran churches of the area are trying to minister to the inner city and to the society of which they are a part. Old truths must continually be applied in new and fresh ways to maintain the vigor and witness of a reformation faith begun 450 years ago, but very much alive today, even within the Roman church.

A survey of some thirty-five to forty brochures produced by Roman Catholic churches in Connecticut in the celebration of their anniversaries shows their similarity to Protestant anniversary celebrations. Varied as they are in their programs, all of them denote the serious business of religion. Even social get-togethers, dances, and dinners are held against a background of serious responsibility for school, church expenses, Christian vocational challenge, and Christian outreach. Often the anniversary is a time for consolidating work which is under way, dedicating some new building project, ground breaking or laying the cornerstone for a school, or renovating the church structure.

The high point of the Catholic anniversary celebrations

is the series of thanksgiving masses, the masses for the departed, and the bringing of congratulations through printed messages and in person by church dignitaries. The Pope usually has a warm, challenging, congratulatory message for the church which has attained a milestone in its history.

The heart of the celebration is thanksgiving to God for his the prayers are deeply expressive of this gratitude and dedicaleadership and guidance of forebears. The mass and some of tion to the work which lies ahead. The following are expressions from the missal:

PRAYER
OF THE DEDICATION OF A CHURCH

"O God, each year we commemorate the dedication of Your holy temple, where daily we celebrate these sacred rites. Graciously hear the prayers of Your people and grant that all who implore Your blessings in this church may joyfully receive the favors they ask. Through our Lord Jesus Christ, Your Son, who lives and rules with You, in the unity of the Holy Spirit, one God forever and ever.

"O God, You invisibly uphold all creation, and for the salvation of mankind. You manifest your might with visible signs. Let this church reflect the power of Your presence, and comfort and bless those who gather here to seek Your mercy in their tribulations. Through our Lord." [8]

SECRET PRAYER

"Graciously hear our prayers, O Lord (and grant that all who are gathered in this church to celebrate the anniversary of its dedication may please You by their complete service of body and soul). May the gifts we offer You help us to attain Your eternal rewards. Through our Lord.

"O God, author of the gifts we here consecrate to You, bless this house of prayer so that all who call upon You in this church may feel the help of Your protection. Through our Lord." [9]

POSTCOMMUNION PRAYER

"O God, from living and chosen stones You prepare an everlasting dwelling place for Your majesty. Hear the prayers of Your people who call upon You and grant that the material growth of Your Church may be accompanied by a deepening spiritual development in her. Through our Lord.

"O Almighty God, in Your mercy hear the prayers offered in this place of worship which we, despite our unworthiness, have dedicated to Your name. Through our Lord." [10]

In none of the anniversaries, Protestant or Catholic, does there seem to be any desire for escapism or retreat to the past. There is a lively acceptance of the present and the future challenge. There is a strength in remembering those of the past, their struggles with successes and failures, their courage, and sacrifice. There is rejoicing that they solved their problems back then, but there is a realistic facing of the fact that the problems of today must be solved today with strength and resolution. The present generation cannot depend upon those of the past to do their work today. The people of today are stronger to confront the problems of today because those of yesterday are a cloud of cheering witnesses.

Looking back over the years, those times seem more calm and serene than today. The people's roots seem deeper. They expected to remain in their homes and towns throughout their lifetime. Walter Lippmann has pointed out that today is different, that every human relation, whether of parent and child, husband and wife, worker and employer, moves in a different circumstance. In fact, we have changed our environment more quickly than we know how to change ourselves.

There can be strength in remembering. Strategy and sophistication can be discerned in the struggle of yesterday; and assurance can be found that current problems are not insurmountable with God's guidance today and tomorrow.

The religious dedication and intent of the three hundred years-old First Baptist Church of Boston took on tangible goals in this Anniversary Resolution which was printed in their anniversary booklet.

ANNIVERSARY RESOLUTION

"Mindful of our inheritance of three hundred years of history we, the present-day members of the First Baptist Church of Boston are resolved to keep faith with those valiant souls of the past who endured suffering in the struggle for freedom to worship according to their own conscience. We resolve also to renew our commitment to Christ, whose call to freedom is the same yesterday, today, and forever.

"We shall endeavor to implement this resolution by projecting into the future the Christian spirit of daring through renewed commitment to the cause of freedom in our own time. We understand that we are called to freedom by Christ today when we assume responsibility for witnessing to the gospel in the following specific ways:

The Witness of the Blue Hill Christian Center
The Witness of Andover Newton Theological School
The Witness of a new church in a new frontier
The Witness of ministry to the aging"

Notes

[1] John W. Brush, "Writing Histories of Three New England Churches," *Baptist History and Heritage,* Vol. II (January, 1967).

[2] Roland H. Bainton, "Book Review," (unpublished) June 14, 1966.

[3] Eula Kennedy Long, "Brazil's Methodists Celebrate Centennial," *Christian Century,* October 11, 1967, p. 1298. Copyright 1967 by Christian Century Foundation. Reprinted by permission.

[4] Gaius Glenn Atkins, *The Anniversary of Your Church,* pamphlet produced by the Congregational Christian Historical Society, 14 Beacon St., Boston, Massachusetts 02108.

[5] Morgan Phelps Noyes, *Prayers for Services* (New York: Charles Scribner's Sons, 1934), p. 216.

[6] Walter Rauschenbusch, *Prayers of the Social Awakening* (Boston: Pilgrim Press, 1909), pp. 134-135.

[7] Samuel H. Miller, *Prayers for Daily Use* (New York: Harper and Row, Publishers, 1957), p. 117.

[8] *Saint Joseph Daily Missal and Hymnal* (New York: P. J. Kenedy & Sons, 1966), p. 1214. Used by permission.

[9] *Ibid.,* p. 1217.

[10] *Ibid.,* pp. 1218-1219.

Appendix

LETTER 1.
ANNOUNCEMENT OF THE COMING ANNIVERSARY

Dear Church Member and Friend:

Our church was founded in ——— and we shall be coming to the anniversary year in a few weeks. Before that time it would be of great help if you would do some thinking and praying on how we might most fittingly remember those who have gone before.

Soon the boards and committees will be formulating plans to provide a joyous and significant year of remembrance. These plans will be only as good as their ability to capture your imagination and excite you with their significance. So this is an invitation to you to take a backward look and see whence we have come as a church fellowship.

Be assured we are not only concerned with the past as a fact, but we are interested in lifting the quality of our witness today and getting prepared for a greater work for Christ in the future.

If some of your family or friends have programs, pictures, or special mementos, please gather them together.

Above all, let's have fun as we look to the past to get a better aim for the future.

Sincerely,

Pastor or Anniversary Chairman

LETTER 2.
REQUEST TO SERVE ON THE ANNIVERSARY COMMITTEE

Dear ________________________:

Will you be willing to work on the Anniversary Committee? As you know our church was founded in __________ and during the next few months we shall prepare for the anniversary year.

Our organizational meeting will be announced in the near future. In the interim, will you be alert concerning how other churches, other denominations, and even churches in other parts of the country have celebrated their anniversaries?

We have some copies of the book, *Celebrating Your Church Anniversary,* in the church library. You may like to look through it for suggestions and study of anniversaries in connection with our local opportunity. I'm sure we can have an interesting time ahead.

Sincerely,

Chairman, Anniversary Committee

LETTER 3.
GRATITUDE FOR ACCEPTANCE OF ASSIGNMENT ON COMMITTEE

Dear __________:

Thank you for agreeing to work on the Anniversary Committee. The first meeting is scheduled for ____________________________ and we hope you can be there. If for some reason you cannot attend, will you please appoint someone to take your place and represent your group?

It is extremely important to have every group of the church represented as we make detailed plans for a fitting celebration.

Sincerely yours,

Chairman, Anniversary Committee

LETTER 4.
APPEAL FOR FUNDS FOR THE ANNIVERSARY

Dear Members and Friends:

An item of faith was put into the budget this year. It was the $0000.00 for the observance of the Anniversary Year.

Little has been said until now of the needs that such an observance entails. It can be as little or as much as the church people and friends desire.

Our Board and Cabinet will do the best creative thinking they can to lay plans that will adequately express our appreciation to the past and our hope for the future.

We really don't have to do anything . . . no one will judge or condemn. However, our leadership thinks we can make something very significant of the many emphases this year. We need evangelism; we need a new thrust in mission; we need a renewed spark and zest in doing the work of Christ in this place. We need a more august sense of worship, and a deepening of the meaning of fellowship.

What will these gifts be used for? For publishing the history of those who have worked and given so generously in the past. Guests will be invited to rejoice with us in paying tribute to those into whose labors we have entered.

Special speakers, travel expenses, publicity, and many other gracious gestures could also be listed . . . but . . . understandably your trustees and church leaders hesitate to make firm commitments until you have had a chance to express your opinion.

We wait on you now. If you desire that we grasp firmly the opportunities of this anniversary year; if you want us to use our best effort and use this occasion for lifting our Christian endeavor to higher levels . . . use the enclosed envelope. Enclose a check or cash gift to salute the past and prepare better for the future.

Thank you for your encouragement. We pledge you our best thinking and planning for a fitting celebration.

Sincerely yours,

FOR THE TRUSTEES *FOR THE CABINET*

LETTER 5.
INVITATION TO CHURCH MEMBERS AND FRIENDS TO ATTEND ANNIVERSARY BANQUET

Dear Member and Friend:

This is your special invitation to a Birthday party. It is the Birthday party of ____________________ Church.

____________________ years ago a group of earnest Christians formed themselves into a church to worship God, teach his precepts, and seek to witness to him throughout the world.

You are a part of that thrilling history. Will you come to pay tribute to those of the past who have given so much?

We look to the past to get a better perspective on the present and, we hope, a better aim for the future. Please help the cause of Christ by being present on ____________________.

Please reply on the enclosed, stamped (card or letter), by ________. Make checks payable to ____________________. Thank you.

Cordially,

Chairman, Anniversary Committee

(Card or letter to be returned. Cross out the statement that does not apply.)

Please reserve _____ places at the Anniversary Dinner and Banquet.
Sorry, we cannot be present.

Name ____________________ Tel. ______________

LETTER 6.
LETTER OF THANKS TO ALL ANNIVERSARY WORKERS

Dear Anniversary Worker:

Please accept the heartfelt thanks of your anniversary chairman and pastor for the recent events which are now history. We have seen the value of the contributions, material and spiritual, which have been poured into our fellowship.

Your thinking, planning, and work of the past weeks and months have borne fruit and we have enjoyed a fitting celebration. We are stronger to face the present and encouraged to face the uncertain future unafraid.

Truly, a part of the work is finished, but there is much yet to do. We are stronger and more ready for what may come.

Do you feel a sense that there is a great cloud of witnesses interested in our striving, our decisions, our Christian living of these days? We do, and we thank you for helping to create that feeling. May God bless you and continue to make you a blessing.

Sincerely,

Chairman, Anniversary Committee

Pastor

ANNIVERSARY ANALYSIS OF FOUR CHURCHES

	1-100th	2-150th	3-50th	4-150th
History researched and written, published	yes	partly	yes	yes
Pageant prepared and produced	no	no	yes	no
Historical display	no	no	yes	yes
Monthly emphases	no	no	yes	yes
Costume evening	no	no	yes	yes
Anniversary banquet	yes	yes	yes	yes
Publicity				
Local (newspaper)	yes	yes	yes	yes
State (denominational)	yes	yes	yes	yes
National (denominational)	no	no	yes	yes
Liturgical art exhibit	no	no	yes	yes

Any unique feature	Citations of church workers	Anniv. dinner plate	Horseless carriage display	Controversial films shown
Photos taken	no	yes	yes	yes
Long range goals	no	partly	no	partly
Pictorial directory	no	no	no	yes
Evaluation	good but limited	good but limited	excellent	excellent
Changes to make another time	Monthly emphases	Write detailed history	none	More ecumenical participation
Financed	Sponsors	Coin banks	Coin banks	Special gifts & sale of histories
Other	Week of Anniv. emphasis	Week of Anniv. emphasis Anniv. hymn	Several highlights during year	Sponsored Indian student study Special preacher Taped addresses Entertained state conv. License to preach Gave awards

Suggestion for SPECIAL OFFERING ENVELOPE
(Size and suggested copy)

Small
picture
of church

1800 1900 (dates)

"Hats off to the past; coats off to the future."
"From heroic struggle to daring renewal," etc. (Anniversary motto)

NAME OF ANNIVERSARY FUND

(Name of Church with complete address)

Name .... (of donor)

CHECKLIST

Below is reproduced a checklist which, if followed by the church now, will provide the basis for the historical account which will be prepared in the next century. Certainly any church will have the blessing of the historian then when he has materials at hand; facts which are stated with accuracy convey to another century the quality and significance of the Christian fellowship now.

How very important this longest of long-range goals could be!

CONGREGATIONAL CHRISTIAN HISTORICAL SOCIETY

14 Beacon Street, Boston, Mass. 02108

Checklist for a Historical Inventory of a Local Church
Prepared by
Prof. Ford L. Battles, Pittsburgh Theological Seminary
Rev. Arthur E. Wilson, Beneficent Church, Providence, R.I.

A. How the records of the Church are kept
   1. Give a description of the official records of your Church, including dates, scope and comprehensiveness, physical condition, and place of deposit.
   2. Are any important records missing? Details?

B. A Critique of Existing Histories, published and unpublished
   1. Give bibliographic descriptions of published books and articles.
   2. Assemble and describe unpublished papers on the history of the Church.

C. Collections of Historical Material having to do with the history of the Church and the community which it serves
   1. Church reports, bulletins, handbooks, membership lists, etc. (date these as accurately as possible)
   2. Clipping files of newspaper articles, etc., dealing with the Church, its members, and the community
   3. Personal collections: diaries, letters, books, etc., in private homes
   4. Collections pertaining to the Church which exist outside the community (in libraries, personal collections of families which have moved away, etc.)
   5. "Secular" histories, local or sectional, that are helpful in reconstructing the parish history
   6. Early street maps, and directories and almanacs
   7. Plan for collecting, copying, calendaring and preservation of such materials.
   8. Early travel books particularly on New England, such as As-

bury's Journals, and Timothy Dwight's "Travels in New England and New York"

D. What to save of current and future materials?
   1. Areas of Church life and activity to be covered in a definitive history:
      a. doctrine
      b. devotional life; worship
      c. educational activities; ancillary organizations
      d. membership and discipline; finance
      e. relationship to other churches and to the community and denomination
      f. biography of clergy and laity
   2. What current written materials should be preserved in each of these areas?
   3. What historical data, not adequately covered in written materials, should be "minuted," and by whom? Taped interviews with older members; transcriptions

E. Archival Policy and Responsibility
   1. Preservation and microfilming of documents: principle—the most important documents to be reproduced and kept in two separate locations
   2. Deposit of Records in Libraries
      a. State Library; local library, historical societies
      b. institutional libraries
      c. denominational libraries
   3. Report of Location, Character and Scope of Documents to Congregational Historical Society
   4. Responsibility: division of labor between church clerk and historian

F. Prepare Now for the Historians of 2063 A.D.
   1. Appoint a Church photographer. Label pictures on back.
   2. Keep a card file of members by the year received, in addition to alphabetical list.
   3. Have a historian's card file on the offices held by members and their activities (commendable) beyond the church.
   4. Keep running lists of principal officers such as deacons, Sunday school superintendents, etc.
   5. Keep a detailed account of repairs and alterations to the church property. In 2063 they will ask "When were the pews changed?", "When was the additional piece of land purchased?", "When was the blue paint that you find underneath several other coats used?"

6. Keep representative copies of the sermons of each pastor. Sermons for special days such as Children's Day, Christmas, etc., are useful for comparison over a century. Be sure to preserve literary efforts of both ministers and members.
7. When a new organization is formed in the Church, record in the historical notes what its purpose is, age groups, etc. Much time has to be spent in unravelling the mystery of organizations of a century ago.
8. Photograph neighboring buildings every few years, and any buildings which are to be demolished. Date and label all pictures, news stories, and everything else.
9. Note damage to Church property by storms or unusual catastrophes.
10. Note local events of an unusual nature: big fires, quadruplets, tragedies, scandals, violent political debates or upheavals, change in manner of government, fire fighting, etc. A church's life is part of a community, and events in each explain the other.
11. Note physical changes in community; new and abandoned roads and streets, how and why named. Change in public transportation.